To Fiona

I'm sure you will enjoy this book of poems.

Best Wishes

Paula.

tonguetied publications

If rays of sun are shining
then the track is where to be
If rain and hail and storm persist
just watch the punters flee....

Tongue tied and blinkered-he's one savage ride
he'll pull you to shreds boy, then cart you out wide

He'll buck so be careful, but don't give him up
for next year we'll bring back that Cheltenham
Gold Cup!

The First Step

Kingston Blount Point To Point
May 1982

I wake up every morning if I can at half past six

That's now pending if I've had a drop to drink

And I sit astride my four year old, our little 'Bob's Return'

And as we trot on up the lane I start to think…

'What is life and where's it going, who am I to really judge?

Will I ever get the chance to have a say?'

Then he gives a little buck as if to simply say to me

'At least you have the chance to fight another day'

Dedication

To the horse boys of Crystal Creek, Zimbabwe

On February 9th 2000, another white owned farm in the heart of the Chimanimani mountain range was struck upon by Robert Mugabees War Veterans as part of the land reclamation programme. Our stay was ultimately and sadly cut short. The memories however, will never leave.

'Where ever you are now, I hope your laughter still rings as clear, and that your work continues to churn out a polocrosse team worthy of world championship status-This is for you lads'

With Special thanks.....

Philip Von Borries. It was in the introduction of your book *Racelines* that got me thinking *'if you write on any subject long enough, you're going to want to do a book on it sooner or later'*! Many thanks for the encouragement and direction, here's hoping there's more to come.

Willy Neville. For the hours of advice and to that memorable winning ride in Cork on Mykon Gold in 2002. Mr Hourigan-I knew you were a little nervous that day but believe me, it wasn't a patch on what I was going through...

To Ray Kennedy for a brilliant artistic display throughout the book-I still chuckle when I see a cartoon of my posterior peering out of the hawthorn

Mum and dad. For the patience and agony you surely endured over the last year. You never stopped believing in me.... thank you x

Triona & Paula-Cheers

To Everyone Else Reading.....Enjoy

tonguetied publications
ISBN 0-9546401-0-1
First Published in 2003 by tonguetied publications
Naas, Co Kildare, Eire

E-mail: beckysurman@hotmail.com
web: www.horsehomour.com   www.tonguetiedandblinkered.com
Copyright Rebecca Surman 2003
Illustrations Ray Kennedy 2003
The moral right of the author and illustrator has been asserted

Second Edition 2003
Printed by Leinster Leader Ltd.
Naas, Co. Kildare

Introduction

A witty collection of true life experiences based on the many characters and places within the hormonal world of horse racing, by award winning poet Rebecca Surman

'May the unfortunate individuals who fell victim to the following creations not be offended by the public invasion of such periods of misendevour-at least you were spared the agony of having a horse named after a certain part of the anatomy viciously massacred by a hungry looking hawthorn'

Well bred

My dad's a true believer-if you wanna breed the best
you need a mare of quality forget about the rest
I see these words ring true now as I'm looking at my mum
for she bred a winning daughter and a pair of cracking sons

Contents

I'm too heavy for a jockey so I struggle with my weight
And no matter what you feed me I shall leave it on my plate

I cycle, swim and starve myself to loose a pound or two
And when I cannot sweat no-more you'll find me on the loo!

A Fathers Advice

'*Now Son*-that's a fine looking filly
just look at the way she moves
A good loping stride-boy she'd give you some ride
and she'd skip through the mud with those hooves

She's a great looking head on that body
what a shape from her tale to those ears
I'd say she can jump-with that muscular rump
what a wonderful case of a rear

And those legs son are strong and yet shapely
and just look at that powerful chest
She's a nice sort of stamp-would go well in the damp
and she'd always be giving her best

She's the breeding-just look at that black type
what a dam line and leading hunt sire
If she went to them sales-man she'd out bid those males
lord-I wouldn't mind being her buyer

But she's tough son and that is essential
a pure athlete-I'd say she could stay
She'd win you a race-say a three mile chase
come out fighting the very next day

But what are you looking for sonny
to race now or mainly to breed?
To sprint or to stay-a grey, blond or bay
and then there's the question of feed

So when choosing a nice looking filly
choose wise and you'll have her for life
Wow-there goes that mare-god I can't help but stare
ain't I lucky that filly's me wife'!

The Perfect Cure

With a sickness in my stomach
and a pain inside my head
It's that monday morning feeling
that was only made for bed

The alarm has failed to wake me -
busy snoring on the floor
I've a cut above my left eye
where I walked into the door

A call from some way down the stairs
'you're half an hour late'
Grab my jodhpurs wet from yesterday
my jackets on the gate

The fridge defrosted overnight
the milk's like cottage cheese
Some chancer nicked my cigarettes
'Jesus-where's my keys'?

Been quicker driving in reverse
stuck with Paddies cows
My newly pebble dashed green car
now joined by Murphys sows

They knew I had a hard night
for the grins across the yard
The boss just blew his rocket
left his whiskers black & charred

Missed riding out the first two lots
black markered by my name
'Go saddle up that wall eyed colt
-he's feeling pretty game'

I slump into the saddle
where he gave a mighty buck
My balance now shot through the wall
I landed in the muck

Re-mounted with my pride disgraced
we head up to the plain
I cross the reins down on his neck
and grab onto his mane

I let him take a good firm hold
and set him to his role
Six furlongs of a rising hill
is sure to calm his soul

The freedom that we feel right then
the two of us as one
No words were needed either way
just watch that breaker run

I pull up with my head now free
a buzz that's cleared the fur
you have your fry or aspirin dose
I've found my perfect cure...

The Perfect Cure…

Sales Day

Vendor	Potential Buyer
She's a cracker	*Chestnut filly!..*
Nicely finished	*Very small*
Smashing dam line	*Where's the black type*
Will I ring you?	*Not at all!*
She's a walker	*Can she gallop?*
Easy mover	*Stuffy stride*
Win a bumper	*Say a flapper*
Cheltenham prospect	*Pony Ride*
She's for selling	*More for giving*
Major interest	*No one here*
She's vintage	*Stick to keg mate*
Glass of Champers	*Pint of beer!*
Selling shortly	*If you're lucky*
Will you bid sir?	*Think I'll duck*
See you later	*At the bar mate*
One for health so?	*Ten for Luck!...*

'Sweet Music'
by Bach out of Game On

Runhimforthemrs...

Trainer *He's no good, a real yolk Mick-a humping great clout*

Owner We'll 'ave to run him for the Mrs for she wants the day out
and she's just gone and bought this expensive new hat

Trainer *But Mick he is useless-more meat on a rat*
and the ground goes against him-I tell you no lie
and the jockey wants out so he's gone to Dubai

Owner Well just run the olde beggar coz she won't let it be
then we'll say he broke down, got a leg or a knee

then she'll see for herself when he runs like a crock
but least she won't ask for another new frock....

A young Trainer from Co Kildare
lived life with such passion and flair
he rode filly on filly but felt a bit silly
when dumped by a crabby olde mare

'Lovely Jubbly'
by Hubbly Bubbly out of Del Boys Girl

'Drop the Hand'
by Lend a Hand out of Sure Thing

'Under the Hammer'
by Talkin Man out of Bid me Quick

Weatherbys DNA Lab

'Where's that bleeding passport
wanna sell that cracking foal?
I swear that mob in Johnstown-
gone to ground and dug a hole

And what about those swab results-
that mare's to go to stud?
I say-if I don't hear today
I'll draw some human blood'!

But listen here you farmers-
stud owners-racing yards
I've proof the crew in Weatherbys
are working ruddy hard!

Extracting blood and DNA
from all your foals and mares
whilst dipping samples into tubes
and cutting little hairs!

And their job would be much easier
if samples sent were clear
and hair is pulled out from the mane
not yanked out from the rear!

All blood must be extracted
and sent up straight away
not stored aside for weeks on end
or mixed with bits of hay!

And there's no use swapping samples
for we're always gonna tell
that your foal is just a half bred type-
no son of Saddler's Wells

So next time you should ring us
please mind your Q's and P's
coz you'll get your equine passports
compliments of Weatherbys

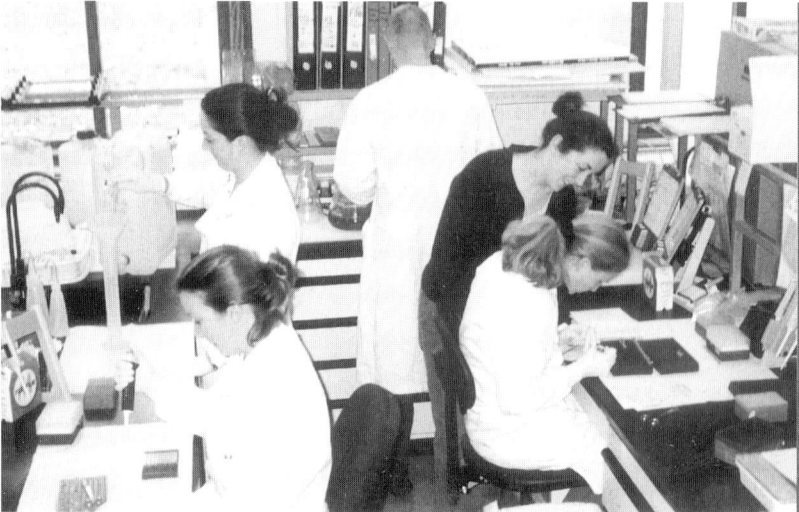

The Weatherbys Crew

Songs for Owners

Heartbreaker~Dion Warwick
Still haven't found what I'm looking for~U2
To Win Just Once~The Saw Doctors
Like A Fool~Blue

A Bargain Buy

Farmer.. *'I wanna buy a mare-nothing fancy nothing flash*
I've had a bad year selling spuds & haven't got much cash

I'm not looking for marello, vintage tipple or dawn run
I just wanna find meself a mare & have a little fun'

Agent.. *'I know exactly what you mean but who are you to kid-*
won't buy a half share in a leg for just a hundred quid'!

Farmer.. *'Now listen here young del boy-I know how you lot think*
you bleed poor fellers like me dry to squander it on drink!

So just take these copper pennies son before I start a row
and get out there and find that mare with strength to pull a plough'!

The door slams shut in johnny's face, he's left there standing dumb
one mother of all missions here-*'I do require a rum'!*

He slips into his local for he needs sometime to think
searching hi and low through books and ads-he hears *'another drink?'*

'Oh why not Jo-the same again, that man is very shrewd
and why you're there-a pack of fags, I'd say it's time for food'!

By now the funds are falling and he's feeling like a rookie
no luck with mares inside the pub-he slips into the bookies

A change of plan was needed for he knew that dreaded fate
to land back empty handed-he'd be shot right through the gate

'This tip I have's a winner so I'll have a little bet'
well you should have seen the finish as his joy turned into sweat

For the photo turned against him as he sat and took his breath
no horse and no more money *'I'll be struck or stoned to death!*

Now I'm really in the horrors-someone take me to the pub
I'll tab a final triple whiskey and a little bit of grub

For I know my life is over-I don't want another row
didn't find a mare for breeding or a shire for his plough'!

So poor johnny down and broken starts to head back to the farm
unaware of on the roadside came to be his lucky charm

For the sight that stood before him made his cheeks turn deep and pinker
for there she stood, a cracking mare led up by fred the tinker

Fred.. *'folk tell me you're the buyer for this lovely looking mare*
you're lucky coz I'm on me way to sell her at the fair

but I see your cause is needy so I'll tell you of my deal
I'll trade this cracking filly for your lovely set of wheels'

Well old johnny couldn't argue for she was a mighty beast
and the pro's weighed out the cons somewhat-from breathing to deceased

So the rope was handed over-couldn't think of what he'd done
'Lord she'd better do the business-bring the farmer all this fun'

Well the farmer was delighted-*'boy I'll say she'll pull me plough*
but I've changed me mind so take her back and swap her for a

cow'!.......

A Bargin Buy

Down in the Sauna

Down in the sauna at our local one in Naas
it's filled with little jockeys sweating buckets from their face

There's Terry, Mark and Harry, Jimmy, Sammy, Will and Hue
olde Johny's down there twice a week to loose a pound or two

Young Robbie lost his claimer so he's busy munching cake
whilst Terry's down there every night-he's strung up like a rake

Poor Billy took a mighty fall just days ago at Tip
so he's sweating out the excess booze while resting up his hip

You should hear their little stories they do tell amongst the steam
how Mandy took a six length lead-she's riding like a dream

And that Betty gives a feeling with a smooth majestic stride
young Sally is that little mare they all would love to ride

But you know these little fillies they do coax along the rails
are not the ones with floppy ears or bushy manes and tails

But the frisky little fillies who will smile and give the look
whilst little jockeys everywhere fall sinker, line and hook

So next time in the sauna you should hear a tale or two
don't back the mare they talk about-young Bessy, Sal or Sue

Coz that pretty mare they boast about and all would love to ride
is the one they'd jump from out the front or take up from behind

(or for those who would prefer a more civil ending)
is the buxom lass with hazel eyes and mighty fine backside!!

At the drop of the flag

'At the drop of the flag-boy get out there and ride
just slot him in nicely-keep on the inside

Stay out of trouble-away from the pack
and don't let him waver or fall out the back

And at those old fences-remember-push on
grip tight with those thighs when you hit it all wrong

Sit deep in the saddle-give plenty of rein
hold tight to his strap and grab onto his mane

There's a sticky wet patch on the very far side
and watch out for the others when riding upside

For that chap on the grey-now he's is all out to win
and he's dirty so watch he don't box you right in

If he's gone-pull him up if he don't like the ground
or the petrol is gone and he's striding unsound

But if you're bang there with just two jumps to go
boy-ride like the wind and remember keep low

For you know he can stay and he jumps like a stag
use the whip like I showed you and don't let him lag

'Now this is your day son-just go rip 'em up
for it's time we brought home that Memorial Cup'

Cheltenham 2002
All Irish Eyes Are Smiling...

Old 'Ned Kelly' said to me
'You'll never Walk Alone'
and you'll fly just 'Like a Butterfly'
from Paris right to Rome

You're sure to hear the 'Chimes At Midnight'
when you're feeling down and blue
but just you stand there 'Big and Bold'
-my son you'll see it through

Though you'll feel an 'Anxious Moment'
as you're standing at the start
those 'Scottish Memories' once recalled
will stay there in your heart

That 'Pearl' you left in 'Florida'
along with old 'Boss Doyle'
he said to you 'Best Wait' my friend
your 'Signature' is 'Royal'

Don't forget now you're my 'Best Mate'
for you fill my life with joy
and 'Heezapistol'-sure to win that
'Ballyhampshire Boy'

As 'Colonel Braxton' talks to you
from right 'Over The Bar'
try 'Alexandra's Banquet'
for his feast will take you far

The 'Moscow Express'-the way to go,
now take another gin
son-live life on a 'Knife Edge'
and those lads will bring us in.....

Owners

Have you heard the common saying that a man is like his dog?
well i'm certain this applies into his horse
for you've owners that are grateful every time their horses run
to the owners who will only show remorse

You have owners who are faithful and will stay with you for life
through the every type of hassle, stress and strain
then you've owners who will turn around & drop you like a knife
then inform you-'you could never really train'

Then there's owners who will hound you-every hour of every day
'howz he doing, when's he running, what and where?'
then you've owners in Morocco who would pay you every day
but when you ring 'em, they are seldom ever there

Take the owners who are clueless but they think they know the lot
try and tell you how to run your flipping yard
and the owners who you wonder if they've lost the ruddy plot
and can not pay you coz your fees are way too hard

And what of owners who appear when you're sitting down for tea
only anxious just to see their Arkle work
& when you tell him that he's bandaged from a rap on to the knee
loose all senses as he screams off in his Merc

From the owners who want action-'get a race in straight away'
though he's come in from the summer full of grass
to the farmer who says nothing and will barter fees with hay
he's bred the gelding who you know is full of class

To the owners that you hear of and you pray will stay away
for they'll cut you if your training is too hard
but it's them who fill your boxes & it's them who make it pay
till you falter then they up and leave your yard

From the owners who just love it for the fun of dressing up
to the homebred nag you just could not refuse
take the owners who aren't happy till you win the Cheltenham Cup
to the owners who are happy just to loose

So you've seen now every owner-tell me which one would be you be
one of happiness, enjoyment or remorse?
just spare a sec now for his trainer-for it's often plain to see
it could be YOU that needs the training not the horse!

Riding

'Now folks I love a good olde *ride* so let me tell you more...
I love to *ride* on two legs but my passion lies on four

for on two legs you need balance and a little bit of luck
coz that two legs starts on four legs-til he starts to scream and buck

but what I hear you ask me is the feeling there on four
well he'll ride you well above the clouds then drop you on the floor

is your preference there in sprinting or a good olde fashion chase
and when you're riding out a finish-is there joy upon your face?

so tell me folks the answer-do you like a good olde *ride*
would you take your mount from out the front or squeeze up the inside?

so why not grab a saddle-do not mock it til you've tried
but when two on two becomes as one-there is no other ride......

I know a young jockey called Terry
whose face was as red as a Berry
one day it turned blue over riding young Sue
so they ended up moving to Kerry

Buying a Horse

one white foot-try him
two white feet-buy him
three white feet doubt him
four white feet out him
four white feet & a blaze down his face
stick him in a rocket-send the begger into space!

My Round..

'If your horse was a beer-tell me what would you take...
a pint of the black stuff-the cream of the cake?
packed full of iron-a body of strength
sure to plough through the field just to win by a length

Or have you a preference for something much lighter..
fizzy as hell but a pure little fighter?
then may I suggest sir this fine apple cider
she may take a strong hold but just get out and ride 'er

If a pint is too much-maybe a wee short
bound to hit the right spot like our hot vintage port
and for those who make all and are packed full of sin
maam-please take a sip of this large double gin

If in need of dutch courage-a single malt whiskey
for you won't feel a thing if he starts to act frisky
give me a great horse who'll be first past the line
so just pour me a glass of your sweetest of wine'

Songs for tearaway horses

Scream if you wanna go Faster~Gerri Halliwell
Opps...I did it Again~Britney Spears
Take Me Home~Sophie Ellis Bextor
Runaway~The Corrs

'Chastity Belt'
by Quws out of No Entry

Assistant Trainer

Assistant Trainer needed
for National Hunt top yard
required to weigh ten stone or less
and work extremely hard

Must use own initiative
appointed head of staff
to chat to owners in the ring
yet joke and have a laugh

To ride with style and confidence
take breakers, school and hunt
with chance to ride in Bumpers
then go and have a punt

Top rates of pay included
with food and digs all in
take every other weekend off
great bonus for each win

So start this stone a rolling
all you grafters do apply
commence this role immediately
no boundary stands too high...

Assistant to Assistant
needed straight away
our last chap seemed to vanish
packed his bags and ran way

You'll share a bunk with Hammid
take turns to sweep and mop
the rent is twenty pound per week
with bills to pay on top

The head lad here is Jimmy
he's deaf and cannot speak
I hope you know some german
five more starting here next week

The yard is pretty empty
I've put em out to grass
we've mainly bad old breakers
that haven't shown much class

You'll get one weekend off a month
I'm sorry if I lied
forget about the license mate
you'll never get to ride

So welcome to our stables son
I think you'll bring us luck
now grab that pike beside you
and get stuck into that muck...

It's All in the Name

Form Guide

Pu	Pulled Up	*couldn't stick the pace*
F	Fell	*landing problems*
U	Unseated	*departure from steed*
R	Refused	*preventing departure from steed*
Br	Brought Down	*similar to above with interference from 3rd party*
D	Disqualified	*non compliance to rules-(made up on day of racing)*
Ro	Ran out	*fence looked dangerous*
Co	Carried out	*was planning to jump but fence looked dangerous to horse on inside*
Wo	Walk Over	*easy money*
1	First	*aim of the game*
2nd		*almost there*
3rd		*still in the prize money*
0	Nowhere	*embarrassment to all connections*

Name of horse	Form

Alien Invader   **U.F.O.** Scary looking individual whose efforts to date merely suggests he's arrived from another planet. Doesn't seem to have the ability to land or take off and has tried to 'abduct' his pilot on more than one occasion. Would not be missed if didn't make a re appearance to the track. Frightening.

Smoke Chain   **Pu.F.F.** Possible wind problems as seems to travel well early on but lacks finishing speed and has been seen fighting for air before making mistakes and falling. Stable also rumoured to be suffering cough. Best watched.

Jordens Assets   **Co.R.R.** Cracking looking filly whose 'black type' breeding would suggest a great career, however the jockey hasn't given her the most encouraging of rides which has been reflected in two poor outings. A change of partner and a better jumping education could see this one back on track!

Strawberry Sponge   Pu.D   Too fat to be any threat at present but all immediate relations have won sweetly and this too looks like a potential customer for better things. One to watch.

Cash It In   Wo.D   An exceptionally well bred individual who was unfortunate to have been disqualified when hot favourite last time out. Entered up for next years spring sales & will surely top the catalogue if present. Will go far.

Bank Loan   1.0.U   Shown serious potential when in top form last season making all to win the Credit Card Championship in Money Haven in July. Since then has encountered horrendous leg problems when trying to hold off 'The Dept Collector' before being unseated in a Chase last time out. Not one to trust.

Emergency Line   9.9.9   Lucky to escape the catastrophe of a five horse pile up last time out in spring of 1999. Not the most fluent of jumpers and doesn't look to safe at present.

Jay F Kay   R.1.P   Dead

Post Race Inquiry Songs

Stewards	Jockeys
Unbelievable~EMF	*It Wasn't Me*~Shaggy
Scandalous~Mystique	*What Would You Do*~City High
Too Close~Blue	*Maybe I'm Right*~Atomic Kitten
Point of View~DB Boulevard	*I'm Sorry*~John Denver

Admiring the View
Lockinge Point to Point

If you take me to the races I will sit and just observe
and I'll pick an each way chance to have a bet
and if he comes in-lord I'll cheer-we shall celebrate with beer
but if the beggar lets me down I'll sit and sweat

Equine Dental Care
Contact: Phil-ling, New-bridge

Lectures

Well I'm sitting in this lecture for the very first this year
& I'm wondering what the hell on earth I'm really doing here

for the words are floating out his mouth and drifting out my ear
& these seats are so uncomfortable-I've pains inside my rear

so I'm sitting in this lecture and I'm thinking-doctor please-
man the only thing I understand is when you stop to sneeze

& your notes on 'equine breeding' seem like high tech Japanese
whilst my thoughts are out the window at that chap down by the
trees

so I'm sitting in this lecture for the only time this year
& I'm thinking of the many ways to get me outer here

then the lad beside me wakes and slowly whispers in my ear
'I think it's time to quit this class and head out on the beer'!

Instructions

Trainer: *'Call yourself a jockey-more a bleeding disgrace*
you rode like a pansy-just cost me that race
I wanted the running-you fell out the back
a gallop I said-not a bloody olde hack
then what did you do-only take him out wide
when I told you the going was on the inside
then up the home straight I wanted Mc Coy
not a sack of olde spuds or a spoilt young boy
If I wasn't t-total I'd be hitting the gin
but you're in the next race-so go bring him in..'

37

Your Loss and Mine

It doesn't matter what they say
-nor the comfort of an arm
when they tell you *'thank the lord-*
you were safe from any harm'!

It's that sickness that you feel
so gut wrenching deep inside
you were travelling there so sweetly
gaining ground with every stride

It was sown up in the bag
as you came up from the rear
that feeling there of cruise control
whilst still in second gear

But the flash back to the fence
oh it happened there so fast
as he came from out of nowhere
cut right through you at the last

Whilst the others found their feet
you had nowhere left to go
the hunter now was hunted
as the string snapped from his bow

As you brushed away the turf
and saw that look deep in his eye
as he tried but failed to find his feet
he blew a painful sigh

You knew from there he'd run his race
he'd sense he'd run no more
though his heart would lift him up
to hear the crowds emphatic roar

As you loosened off the girth
and spoke that softened final word
as you walked away with lowered head
that cringing shot was heard

So-it doesn't matter what they say
when you walk on past that line
for his loss will stay forever
a great loss-both yours and mine.....

That Olde Mare

She won't eat or drink-what more can I do
She kicks and she bites and she's just thrown a shoe

She shakes and she sweats at the drop of a hat
She weaves and she sucks like a vampire bat

She coughs and she paws and she bites at the crib
Don't mention the topic about womans lib

She's broke at the mouth and she's shot in the head
And she's always reluctant to get out of bed

She's knocked at the knees and she's dipped in the back
She refuses to load or ride out on a hack

Though she's many a vice I'm her number one fan
For there's no one like Braidy-my smashing olde gran

Galway 2002

Going good to soft-track is poached
from Dermot Weld to Christie Roche

Johny, Ruby to McCoy
Go Say Again to Rockholm Boy

Guinness tent to Ladies day
just bed 'em up and give 'em hay

Bookies give an each way bet
and watch young Nolan start to sweat

To Nina, Helen-Catherine
I'll drink to you a double gin

And Hadnett still a five pound claim
whilst others pulled up feeling lame

Fallers-jockeys out the door
up the straight the crowd will road

Beaten favourite-bookies cheer
mid division-out the rear

From Ted to Tracey-Robert Hall
there's nothing like that Galway roar....

To Be A Trainers Wife?

I'd love to be a Trainer
and have 'the Trainers life'
the one job though I'd fear the most
to be a *Trainers Wife*

Just picture now a Trainer
sitting with his Racing Post
busy munching on his breakfast
poached eggs on buttered toast

And who had put it there for him
now dishing out some more
the cook of course-his darling wife
now rushing out the door

She changes role-becomes a mum
three tots to take to group
but not before she's walked the dog
let the bantams out the coup

And on return she grabs a fork
and worn out tattered broom
three horses mucked and hooves picked out
'she makes a decent groom'

And when the boss strolls on the scene
she's hacking out the yard
'hey don't forget the entries
the Tipperary card'

When lunch is packed and tail board's up
he flies on down the lane
five minutes break, she takes a seat-
before she goes insane

But not before the phone does ring
you've guessed it-it's the boss
'forgot to say-Bill's on his way-
no time to sit and doss'

For what she thinks-no weekly pay
be lucky for a thanks
'cash problems' he would turn and say
'no money in the bank'

The moral of this story girls-
listen wise and listen well
a Trainers life-more a *'Trainers Wife'*
Just absorb these words I tell...

Should you spot him at the races
looking pucker in his tweed
and he eyes you deep within the crowd-
No doubt his mind will read....

'Can she cook, clean, hay, muck stables
drive boxes, sweep and ride?
be a mother to my children
yet still look fancy on my side'?

Now if he still looks so appealing
and you can handle all the strife
go forth-take on the challenge
and become a *Trainers Wife*-but

There is another option
take both the credit and the strife
go forth-take out a permit
be a Trainer-SOD THE WIFE...

To Be A Trainers Wife?

Racing Thoughts

Commentators review after the last race of the day, the eight year old mares maiden... *'finally pulling up the rear under an exhausted jockey ...Mighty Meg'*

Trainer to Owner She'll be better off after that she needed the run
translation.. *Oh my god...I've been landed another flaming yolk*

Jockey She didn't like the ground boss
nor the course, distance or race

Owner And she was looking and travelling so well in the parade ring
still could have a crack at next years Gold Cup

Horse BLOODY HELL I'm knackered

Trainer I'll stick her in a selling hurdle next time. There's one coming off in a fortnight
best way to get rid of that yolk

Jockey Think I've already a ride in that race boss
better find one quick!

Owner That sounds more appropriate (hasn't a clue)
if she wins-I'll buy a hat for Ascot

Horse Not in my lifetime
Nor my daughters lifetime

A fortnight later after the selling hurdle......
Mighty Meg not looking so mighty now last of the finishers!

Trainer Best let her off now for the summer-she'll come back a different animal next season
let a gun off instead..flaming useless

Jockey She'd be great little mare if she could jump and gallop a tad bit quicker
great in a donkey derby

Owner Indeed-she's definitely shown some potential to work on
maybe the Champion Hurdle in a few years

Horse YES! the green, green grass of home.....

I'm cold and wet and freezing
& it's driving me insane
My hands are numb from riding
& we're heading into rain

It's only tuesday morning
& the flu's gone to my head
Well-bugger this, I'm heading home
& nipping into bed

On The Menu

Waiter: *'Beef or Salmon Mickey or the Special of the Day?'*

Michael: *'I'll have 'em both my dear chap, if you're prepared to pay. I'll have it with a bowl of nuts-a sprinkling of hay And bring him out a chestnut, I don't want no bleeding grey.'*

Sick day

It's half past two on a sunny afternoon
and I'm wondering what the hell on earth to do

But me arm is in a sling and my back is up the creak
-I'm having trouble just to make it to the loo

Me lad has phoned in sick-though I know he's fit and well
while me ma has jiggered off with uncle Fred

I've got sixteen in the yard who are calling out for work
and I'm lying like a knacker in this bed!

I've got bills to make me sweat and I'm plunging into dept
and me head is only beating like a drum

Well the nurse is on his way and i'm certain that he's gay
I dread to think now what he'll stick into my bum

Still-I lie here in this bed, contemplating in my head
I could put the world to right and go berserk

But the racing's on TV-from Down Royal to Tralee
so I thank you lord that I'm too sick to work!

"9-4 the field"

'Ladies and Gents-will you have a wee bet
on this beautiful bank holiday?
for this money could raise you right out of your dept
you can bet for a win or each way'

See Johny up high on his tattered old box
young Lukie is right by the ring
while Terry gives out like he usually does
'this olde pitch you know won't take a thing'!

Now Barry's the gent and he's looking content
as the punters crawl out from the bar
poor Harry missed out on the roll call again
for a tractor crashed into his car

'I'll give nine to four on-so come bet while you can
too late sir-she's now six to four
I'll have ten on the nose and a pound if you may
I'll take sterling, a tonne or a score'

The favourite is beat to the bookies relief
though olde Billy-he had 'em each way
see Sammy has fled and the punters see red
for he hadn't the money to pay

So from Wexford to Naas, from the flat to a chase
see the bookies stand tall on their block
watch the tactics they use for a win, draw or loose
just to get the huge punters to flock

But the life that they lead is not one full of greed
it's enough just to make us both sweat
way up on their towers-from Savage to Powers
on the bookies just take a wee bet

TOO LATE SIR...
SHE'S NOW 6/4 !!!
LUCKY
CON
9/4 THE LASS
BIG BOY
SLOW SAM
FAST EDDY
100/1 - BAR
WHA??
BET WIT
LUCKY CON
CARD

Charlie

A birthday ode to our former Point to Point Jockey and Trainer,
Charlie Morlock of Kingston Lisle, Wantage

Charlie-'*Happy Birthday*'-only 40 years today
I'd say it's time to bring you in and feed you up on hay

Now cast your mind a few years back when you and Doug first met
Whilst riding up the 'Kingston Hill' and working up a sweat

Said Doug to Chris '*I need a chap to ride there in a race-
He'd need to be a good 'en coz my lad will set some pace*'

Says Chris –'*see him from Hendersons-now he's the chap for you*'
And when on '*jack the lad*' you sat, Doug said '*I think he'll do*'

The next time you saw Dougie-I think you will recall
When at Larkhill Point to Point, you took a mighty fall

Well on the scene came Dougie-big grin across his face
'*I can't believe you fell off chap, I backed you in that race*'

Well all that changed at Tweseldown-I can recall it well
For half the field just pulled right up, I'd say the others fell

But when bounding up the home straight, you were still a fleet ahead
I prayed lord '*please don't squander for my pa will just see red*'

Well sure enough you flew by in a flash of blue and white
'*Congratulations Charlie boy-at least you got that right*'!

Since then you've hung your boots up, busy training on the farm
'Above the Cut' and 'Uluru' and watch that 'Native Charm'

So 'Happy Birthday Charlie' for you've shown us all some class
But sad to say-you'll have to wait til you go out to grass

Ballycurragh

'Will you have a cup of tea
and another slice of cake?
& do come on in from out the rain
-you'll freeze for goodness sake'

Now this place that I do speak of
in the Carlow countryside
Is a stud, a farm, a training yard
with breakers there to ride

You'll always get a warm reception-
though prepare to lend a hand
for you'll be knee deep in mucking out
to lunging in the sand

And the Murphy lads will tell you
for they love a good olde yarn
while they sit there on the bales
telling stories in the barn

Whilst now Kortashan and Amylinx
and Plaisir up the way
wait patiently for lunch to come
-a scoop of nuts and hay

Now I won't forget the work force there
of Alan and wee Edd
who get stuck in through rain and hail
with cheeks a-glowing red

Just venture down and see yourself
the massy in the yard
and watch the river flow on through
just like a picture card

Though I've met 'em only recently
I'd say I know 'em thorough
Mrs Murphy, Jim, Noel and Will
the team at Ballycurragh

The Racing Game

It's a funny olde game this racing lark
today you may shine as you step out the dark
But you know that tomorrow could crash to the ground
for not one of your horses is walking out sound

That familiar cough as you stroll down the drive
at a time when you felt they were coming alive
And the star in the yard has only broke down
coz you knew that this feller was going to town

His owners are flying from Rome as we speak
to watch him perform in the Cup there next week
So what will they do when you say he won't race?
how will they act with that look on their face?

It's that time when you feel you could jack it all in
walk away from it all-throw it all in the bin
To make matters worse-the two that are fine
are the nags on the end that are not worth a dime!

And those are the ones that would race everyday
but they're no bloody good and his people won't pay
Your mare's slipped her foal and that sire now is dead
and you're that ruddy tired-you could die in your bed

But-hang on one sec now and just look around
you've a beautiful yard that is worth a few pound
And you know that your dad now like you there before
came just inches away from slamming the door

But he stood his own ground and refused to give in
threw away the old 'Bushmans' and bottles of gin
For he knew that before him-his dad on the wall
had won champion trainer just three years before
And deep in that photo-he read in his eyes:

'Son, your time has arrived so get out there and rise
Just hold your head high and push your way on
for that cough will pass through and they'll soon be on song
And the headlines will read 'you're the man in the light
coz you worked ruddy hard and it's turning out right'

So next time you feel that it's gone in a race
there's a hundred or more who would die for your place
You were born on the scene so jump out of your bed
Son-there's horses to ride and the yard to be fed'!

Only fools work with horses.....

Only fools work with horses-only horses make us sweat
and our sweat will turn to rivers when we loose that winning bet

And if fool just work with horses-how come horses seem to know
that they'll drop us when we're feeling high then life us when we're low

So if fools just work with horses-let me ask one thing of you
why do we keep on letting bleeding horses make us fools?

The Telephone Conversation

Line one 'Hello-this is Sammy at the stud-what can I do?
Oh Mrs Tracy-yes I'm fine thanks what's the story there with you?

Oh that's lovely and how's Mickey-well I'm sure Jo's doing fine
can you hold on just one sec now-someone on the other line?'

Line two 'Terry-can I ring you back-I'm rather in a fix
-yes I said I'd make that order for two tonne of hay and mix

and I'll type that ruddy letter when I get a little time
look-I'll ring you back there later-someone on the other line'

Line one 'Mrs Tracy-I am sorry, things are getting pretty mad
yes I heard your neighbour passed away that's really very sad

And you bought a little kitten-shall I pop in after tea?
did you hear that Cathy had a boy-that's baby number three

Well it really was a pleasure, now I've heaps of work to do
Oh your mare now Mrs Tracy-well I haven't got a clue

What's her name-you can't remember-does she have foal at foot?
now you say she may be barren-either white or black as soot!

Mrs Tracy-don't you worry-I shall find out straight away
yes I see now she's a maiden and she's definitely grey

It says she's still in training and is entered down to race
in the maiden there this afternoon just up the road in Naas

They say she's pretty fancied so I'll just sip up my tea
grab your bag and boots and betting slip-I'll pick you up at three'!

Monty

Now folks will you listen to this chirpy little tale
set within the luscious dairy countryside
for it recalls of the glory where so many try but fail
but for one horse-it was merely just a ride

It had always been a dream, but for those at Curraheen
a burning passion grew within them deep inside
for on that chilly April morn, just before the break of dawn
this famous trip began with Mary by his side

Now forget the dickybow, for up the road from Ballynoe
good olde Jimmy packed his bag and made his bed
and with Mossy by his side-he kissed the twins and Jane goodbye
'don't forget there's other horses to be fed'

Whilst they tried to keep it cool-from the stands of Liverpool
Mr Futter had his faith right from the start
for he had a little bet-just to make the bookies sweat
but by four o clock that day they ate their heart

Now this wasn't just a race, it 'twas the greatest steeple chase
and the buzz it was electric in the crowd
Barry rode him with such flair, over beeches and the chair
and you boys you really did the Irish proud

And from the elbow to the straight-bring on Arkle or Best Mate
for he had 'em really flat right to the core
and when you came on past the post-to you Monty we will toast
the cheer was deafening Carlow to Tramore

Well they partied till the dawn and missed the ferry in the morn
but that did nothing as the crowds came out to gork
from the Curragh down to Tip-the whole of Ireland seemed to rip
it surely bust the seams inside the heart of Cork

And from the 'Winners' to the 'Rest' Gina sang 'Simply the Best'
and the dance it really rocked right through the night
and if I really stop to think, what from the dancing to the drink
I could tell you-we were not a pretty sight

I'll take my hat off to your win Mary, Jimmy, Shirley, Linn
and that stripy woollen cosy full of class
but the hero of the day is now munching on his hay
from us all we really thank you-*Montys Pass*

Healy Racing

Pee Stop

Sunday 10am, the morning after the night before, heading towards
the races down a rickerty old road...

Lass Jack please stop-I'm busting...jeez I'm dying for a pee

*Driver You know I'd love to stop dear Kate, but first race starts at
three-and if I don't get there straight away, you know the boss will
curse*

Lass but surely you must understand-my bladders gonna burst

So just to keep the silence poor olde jack pulls off the road
and young Katie now in agony hops off just like a toad

You can picture now the story for as sure as night is black
the boss appears and gives poor Jack a full blown heart attack

*Boss I knew I couldn't trust you Jack, you're sleeping on the job
and where the hell is Katie, you've no time to act the yob*

So let this be a lesson if you're dying for a pee
and you're heading down a bumpy road and can not find a tree

Do not drink a fleet of water-over do it on the saurce
for now Jack will never stop off til he hits that ruddy course

Garvan 'Red lad' Donnelly

What a fine upstanding chap he is
just see that glowing head
the 'Carrot Man' of Arthur Moores
-pure chestnut thoroughbred

I hear he's dubbed the 'Head Lad'
the best there's ever been
though more than once he's been caught
out with dirty magazines

And is this true-his tendency
to go quite mad and strip?
and venture down to Haydens Pub
then head out on the rip?

He took a spin a few years back
on Northern Galaxy
poor Punchestown went up in smoke
for 'Red' was running free!

But fair play to the main man
for he took that Bumper Race
though next time he got brought to ground
by loose 'en's up in Naas

Since then he's hung his leathers up
been training eve since
his pride lies in his 'pointing lad'
the one he calls the 'Prince'

So take this word I write to you
-although you are a whinger
we thank the lord he made you red
-for we love a bit of ginger

The 'Red Lad' & Ben Delmer
Part of Arthur Moores Workforce

I'm a woolly little chaser
and I stand at sixteen hands
I've won a good few races
- over twenty seven grand

They tell me I'm too old now
and my racing days are through
so they're sending me to Bangladesh
and turning me to glue

Songs for Trainers

Switch~TLC
Keep the Faith~Bonjovi
Stay with Me~Shakespears Sister
Busted~Matchbox Twenty

Derryair

We've a chaser back home little 'Derryair'
how we named him will surely amuse
for he wasn't the safest of jumpers
and would often duck out or refuse

It was dickens job just to school him
my instructions were merely *'sit tight'*
when he jumped what was there just before him
he would rapidly veer to the right

Well-this one day I clearly remember
as we took on these telegraph poles
he was hitting them left, right and centre
trying to bury me deep in a hole

Well I sat there and prayed he would clear 'em
this was heading the shape of a pear
when he shot to the right in his leaping
something shot up my poor derryair

Well-my olde man just roared out with laughter
such a sight that drew tears to his face
as his horse lay ajar in the hawthorn
I just crashed down from galaxy space

And the cushion that broke my poor landing
as I lay facing the sky like a spare
was a pain that I'll always remember
a pain deep in my poor derryair

Well thank god that we managed to cure him
for I'm still feeling quite tender and rare
next time I take on that same hawthorn
I'll just pad up my poor derryair!

Four cracking colts in a muddy old field
'maam, which one would you like to buy'?
'the one with four legs and the handsomest face
and the one that just gave me the eye'!

Page 666 in your Catalogue...

From Suspect Stables
the property of Mr Con Agent

Lot 666

Due to an error in complilation-lot 666 was printed as a blank page. The correct pedigree is now as follows and can be attached to the relevant page in you catalogue. We apologise for any inconvenience this may have caused to any associated connections & hope that this has not affected the sale of the animal in any way

			Busted Vessel
		Supreme Bleeder	
			Red River
	Broken Down		
			Panned Out
Heart Breaker		Free Flow	
(1999)			See the Light
Only Produce			
			Crock **Back**
		Old Splint	
			Shot Gun Sally
	Seldom Sound		
			Full Of **Oats**
		Hot legs	
			Savage Babe
	E.B.F Nominated (Everybody Flee)		

This gelding is well handled and will be driving owners insane by time of sale. Sold with a very expensive Veterinary Certificate
First Dam
SELDOM SOUND (Jp): Unraces-Appropiatley named considering she never touched a racecourse despite six years in training. Died shortly after foaling.
Second Dam
HOT LEGS: **2 Wins** and placed once. **Winner** of 14.2h and under novice flapper and charity race clocking the slowest mile in Ireland this decade. Also ran into hurdles breaking down on last outing. Dam of two winners from two runners:
PIN FIRE LADY: **1 win** (47 Euros). **Winner** of p-t-p 1995 (walkover).Placed once in Charity race won by Hot Legs (2 runners). Own sister to HOSE ME DOWN
SAVAGE BABE. Ran twice on flat & flattened what she ran over hurdles. Dam of 3 winners
SEVERE PACAFIST. Won and placed twice in only 36 starts. Winner of novice ploughing Championship Belgium 1987 Also placed in same event.
OUT OF CONTROL: Won Best Turned out Heinz 57 Class
WALK AWAY: Won Minature pony class at Glastonbury Music festival 1984

STABLED OUTBACK IN FAR SHED
Viewing-Appointment Only!

If I could describe now the way that I feel
I could tell you this one thing for sure
I'd either admit-that's the end of the drink
'orse I'd head to the pub for the cure

A Jockeys Reflection

Now I'm 26 years as a jockey
and I'm thinking of calling it quits
for I've been on my back and I've taken the slack
and my body is really in bits

And I've landed some mighty olde crashes
dislocated both arms and me hip
got done at the line so they gave me a fine
and again for too much of me whip

Been loved and abused and just hated
informed-'*You're a bleeding disgrace*'
and what can you do when they give out to you
when you win them their very first race?

Spent hours upon hours of driving
for my mount to be failed by the vet
and the favourite that day who'd have blown 'em away
didn't run coz the course was too wet

And my body is weak from the hunger
can't remember the last time I ate
cut meself to the bone-just to loose half a stone
'*Yea a jockeys life really is great*'

So I'm 26 years as a jockey
and me body is just like a rake
think I'll give it rest for I gave it me best
and I really could do with a steak..

Charity Race

'Do you fancy a ride in a Charity Race
there's a few coming up here in Cork and in Naas?
He's a right little horse-sure I'll give you a spin
I can picture it now-your first ride with a win'

Well you couldn't have written those words on my face
as I stood there a-shopping in Tescos in Naas
& as I reached for the champers and bottles of wine-
a chill of excitement just shot up my spine

'Jeez-thanks for the offer-I just can't wait to go
my fitness will pump like Sebastian Coe'!
Well-I ran and I jogged and I span down the gym
and I ate all I knew that would help me get trim

But the one thing that brought such a glow to my face
that mechanical horse right inside there in RACE
as I watched those young fellers-all style with the whip
my poor little legs gave away at the hip

When the first day of June did arrive there in Cork
my nerves were a-shot like the pray of a hawk
But the pre-race advice that was given to me-
made me hold my head high and that the hawk set me free

As I togged myself out in that green and red sash
the punters began to depart with their cash
From the leg to the saddle-right down to the start
I felt every beat of my poor little heart

When the starter did call and the tape became slack
the others were turning and holding right back
But we lifted right off to a mighty fine start
it was then that I thought I had swallowed my heart!

As I look back to then-I remember each stride
One mile and five furlongs-he gave me some ride
Though the others tried hard just to keep with the pace
I knew that my feller had control of the race

With just furlongs to go-they tried to draw near
he just picked himself up and slipped into fifth gear
Not a kick or a slap or a flick of the whip
just a squeeze of the heels as we ended our trip

As we shot past the line in such disbelief
my nerve changed from anguish to total relief
I shall never forget that great joy on my face
All thanks to a ride in that Charity Race

Healy Racing

Jockey: *'I'm tellin' you-it's all in the hands'*

Lass: *'Oh come off it'*

Headlines

Headlines in the Post 'Another Track Is Under Threat'
'Some Fella Won a Million With A Single Euro Bet'
'A Jockey Fined For Drinking-Claimed He Didn't Touch A Drop'
'Whilst Another's Under Scrutiny For Riding To A Stop'
'The Grey To Win The Classic-Take The Chestnut For The Cup'
'Two Trainers Out of Fashion-While Another's on the Up'
'A Company Sued For Tampering & Messing With The Feed'
'A Multi Million Stallion-Lost His Mojo-Will Not Breed'
So go on make the headlines if the fame is what you seek
But guaranteed, you'll be wrapped round some fish and chips next week

Little Ride

Carefree colt grazing in a field, experience of man brutal-vaccinated-
wormed-rasped-parred-twiched-you name it, he'd had it! Next stop
castration...this was the one thing he wasn't letting go without a fight...

'RED ALERT! ACTION-FLIGHT
he can try with all his might
I am not gonna let him take my pride
I've felt every type of pain
from my butt into my brain
all I'm asking for is just a little ride!

So he kicks up with his heels
and heads across the other field
while his boss is standing looking like a clown
'HEY YOU- *don't run away*'
but this colt just wants to play
'*think I'm gonna have to shoot this beggar down*'!

Well from the dust into the dawn
that colt ran circles on the lawn
not a bother on his frisky little sole
but as he tried to jump a ditch
he got himself into a hitch
came a cropper as he slipped into a hole

'*Well that serves you bloody right*
you can stay there through the night
for tomorrow I shall take away your pride'
well that silly little colt-
thought he'd gone and shot the bolt
'*now I'll never get the chance to have a ride*'

Well now Jack across the way
phoned the RSPCA
he'd been watching like a hawk now all the while
he'd seen that cracking looking colt
so he threw a pinch of salt
dollars flashing..*'I could make a tidy pile'*

And now Jack-he got that lad
while the farmer felt quite bad
thought he'd sunk into the bog and laid to rest
and he calmed that feller down
and as he rode him into town
his eyes-they sparkled just like rubies from a chest

Now that colt was full of class
though Jack knew it couldn't last
and he ended up confessing to his mate
'best not to rob or steel-try and come to some old deal
if you do now-either leg it or migrate'

Well that colt he went to stud
and they named him 'Stuck In Mud'
and he made his owners smile with joy and pride
but if he hadn't run so far-
his pebbles now'd be in a jar
and he'd never got to have his little ride!

Little Ride

My Little Chestnut Mare

They say she's like a woman
with that spark deep in her eye
Never knowing how to take her
if she's on another high

The only secret to survival
is to play and keep her calm
Then it's safe to say-you'll be ok
and far from any harm

But should you cross her, lord have mercy
may you live to tell the tale
The chestnut female of the species
far more deadly than the male

But my best mate is a red head
and I love my little mare
Wouldn't swap them in a million
or change the colour of their hair

Now I say this loud with confidence
that nothing can compare
To that fiery loon-her name was moon
my Arab, chestnut mare

My fist pony was a rotter
a woolly grey old thing
Wouldn't walk, trot, jump or canter
and would always cut me through a wing

Then we bought this palomino
a fine bargain from stow fair
Though a flashy looking little chap
wasn't chestnut or a mare

Then I saw her on that summers day
appearing from the gate
Was told she was 'unridable'
was destined for her fate

But something clicked between us both
And how could I refuse
With flaxan mane and dishy nose
I had nothing there to loose

At first it all went pear shaped
For she really was a wire
She bucked me clean so many times
I swore I was on fire

But we grew this understanding
And I learnt a thing or two
How to hold the reins like cotton
And to stick like superglue

Our first rosette-what a break through
At our local clear round
Must have jumped that course right inside out
And spent on twenty pound

But from then on-we were flying
For this duo with such flair
Was a farmers lass form Oxfordshire
With her Arab, chestnut mare

And at camp, oh did we show 'em
We were never giving up
Up against those triple barrelled names
We stole 'em of the cup

I now look upon those memories
Like they were yesterday
And smile at all those crazy times
We'd try and runaway

I'm not writing as a red head
For in fact I am quite fair
But this tale recalls of days I spent
astride my chestnut mare

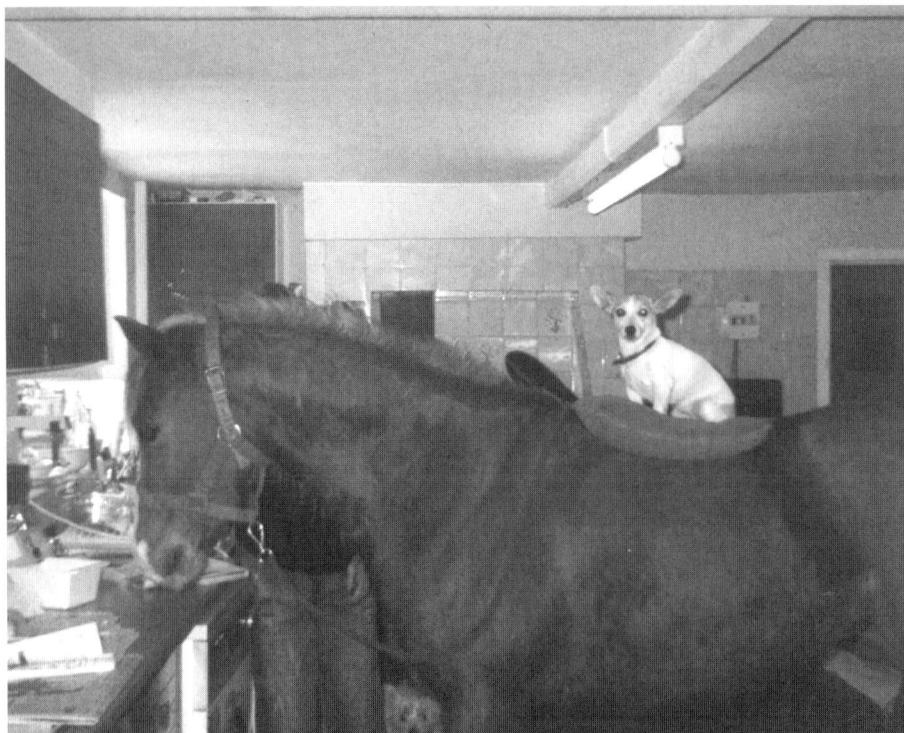

My Little Chestnut Mare

Pony: *'Where's my grub...?'*

Dog: *'Never mind your grub, just get me outta here'*

A frisky young filly Marie
had a body for all men to see
but the length of her stride
gave the fellas some ride
made 'em drool and go weak at the knee

And Finally About Me..

There was this little lassie who would dream aboard her massy
of the day she'll go and win that aintree chase
she believes this will come true-when she buys a mare or two
but for now she'll keep on riding out in Naas

One Year On...*memories of 2002*

On the second day of February-about this time last year
I was back upon the family farm-remembering so clear

Our pride and joy of City farm-our 'Cheltenham horse to be'
was staring out across the yard for all the world to see

We had no high tech rubber track or gallop up a hill
just stubble ground on set-a-side, but man was that a thrill

No open ditch or fancy flight to sail on like the breeze
no-Surmans style was wooden steaks with last years christmas trees

But none the less we got 'em there-our local members race
when mum would lead our feller in with pride upon her face

And those old days will stay for life though deep inside I knew
that time had come for me to tread a path across the dew

So to this day a year ago with hopes and dreams a rye
I packed my little Peugeot car and waved my folks goodbye

For on we set-the world ahead, no boundary stood before
our chance was there to turn the key and open every door

But first we had to set a sail and onward with this load
we dodged the mighty pot holes and the drunkard on the road

The signs were few and far between and often not at all
I felt this land of leprechauns were standing ten feet tall

And when at last we reached our spot-our time had just begun
we'd found the home of Gold Cup dreams-the trainer of Dawn Run

For here we stayed and learnt the ways of riding, muck and hay
whilst over tea and home-made bread-the dreams of yesterday

Well-not long had I been there when the headlines took us out
the nation back in England had been hit with Foot and Mouth

And from that dreaded moment-could have heard a penny drop
as the equine world around us seemed to grind right to a stop

All racing was abandoned and no movement was aloud
the sky began to rumble far above a darkened cloud

One Year On.....

The weeks began to tick on and there sadly was no change
so again we headed onwards to the Coolmore home of Grange

And in the land of Co Cork-the haven of Fermoy
I swapped my role to office work from that of stable boy

And at my desk I scribbled all those permits stacking high
it seemed you needed paperwork for every cough or sigh

But not to be disheartened-those mares kept on flowing through
and the new French star 'The Pistol'-man he knew just what to

And then one day this duo came 'a-strolling' through the door
the pair that stood before me was a sight not to ignore

A woolly hat aboard him-he was sounding rather bossy
why of course it was old Conna man with faithful sidekick Mossy

*'Jimmy Mangan is my name and I hear you like to ride
and this chap here is 'The Manager' a standing by my side'*

From then I took my weekends at his stables up the lane
where we'd muck 'em out & break 'em in through blizzard, storm & rain

And I head the Galway memories just back in ninety seven
when Stroll Home brought the Plate to rest in Conna cloud eleven

If Montys Pass could do the bizz-the bells would surely chime
ran a stormer back in sixth place but the year belonged to Grimes

Well back up in the office, the days so quickly passed
and the season sadly ended so the lads went out to grass

As I printed out the covering certs and posted out the bills
I wondered what adventures lay ahead with many thrills

'Assistant Trainer' caught my eye so pondered on some yards
I wouldn't mind the little pay or working ruddy hard

But I knew that the 'Assistant' or in this case would be true
would be mucking out for most the day and riding out a few

One Year On.....

So I took another option as I drove up to Kildare
swapped my wellies for a lab coat-stuck a comb into my hair

I was heading to the centre of the equine industry
to the blood research and DNA of Mr Weatherby

And though at first I found it hard adjusting to this role
for I'd be at home with mucking out-not testing bits of foal

But I soon got into rhymth and the coat began to fit
so I pulled the reins a tighter-started pulling at the bit

Now I'm standing here now at Cheltenham as a clerk with a bookie
and I watch that marvel run in of Ted Walshes Rince Ri

I still yearn to be a Trainer and win myself a chase
then pull the girth up one more hole and ride a bumper race

As I'm standing here recalling of the last few days gone by
from farm to yard, to stud to lab-I gave 'em all a try

I know I've given everything-if I don't make it here
I'll train back home in Oxfordshire-but that's another year.........

A Little Story

I have a little story
'bout a little lad from Gorey
from the yellow belly Wexford town down there
Well this chap was such a sight
couldn't read or dare to write
And had mats and dreads instead of shiny hair

Well this lad was not a phoney
for when sat upon a pony
Not a teacher could have taught him such a course
When on four legs he did sit
let's just say the suit did fit
Complete with top-hat when he sat astride a horse

Now this lad was not a sinner
and rode winner upon winner
From Down Royal, down to Cork & back to Naas
so next time upon T.V.
you spot a jockey from Gorey
Note-he may not read but jeasus can he race

Songs for Bookies

The Gambler~Kenny Rodgers
Money's Too Tight To Mention~Simply Red
Against All Odds~Phil Collins

Songs for Breaking In Horses

Staying Alive~The Bee-Gees
I Will Survive~Gloria Gaynor
Wild Horses~U2

It is every Jockeys dream to ride a winner and the feeling is truly a magical experience. However, they are faced with unimaginable danger everytime they sit aboard a horse.

Over the past three months in Ireland alone, two prominant Jockeys have fallen victim to the cruel result of an occupation they devote their lives to. Many others have been left with horrific injuries preventing them from ever riding again.

A contribution from the sale of each book will be donated to the Jockeys Accident Fund, to benefit such injured jockeys and to the families of the bereaved.

Further contributions can be made to:
The Kieran Kelly Memorial Trust,

Turf Club, Curragh,

Co. Kildare, Ireland

Forthcoming Books

- *toungetied & twisted (drinking ditties)*

- *tonguetied & broken (It's a Farming life)*

The End . . .